Music is a River of Life

Also by Adrian Rogers and published by Ginninderra Press
The Sun Behind the Sun
Between Two Hemispheres
The Prisoner's Messenger
The Medicine Wheel
Seasons, Situations and Symbols (Pocket Poets)
Human Nature & the Welfare State (Pocket Polemics)
Croagh Patrick (Pocket Places)
Port Victoria (Pocket Places)

Adrian Rogers

Music is a River of Life

Music is a River of Life
ISBN 978 1 76041 658 4
Copyright © text Adrian Rogers 2018
Cover photo : Markus Spiske via Snapstock

First published 2018 by
GINNINDERRA PRESS
PO Box 3461 Port Adelaide 5015 Australia
www.ginninderrapress.com.au

Contents

Introduction	7
The Life River	9
Hildegard of Bingen	11
The Sanctuary	13
Illumination	14
Charles Williams – His Confession	15
Hildegard's Knowing	16
J.S. Bach	17
Et In Arcadia Ego – a Musical Offering	19
The Art of Fugue	20
One Light – after Plato	21
I Tego Arcana Dei – a Musical Offering	22
Mozart	23
The Magic Flute – Persephone	25
The Magic Flute – Pamina and Tamino	26
Symphonic Jupiter	27
A Mysterious Stranger	28
Beethoven	29
Storm Surge – from the 5th Symphony	31
The Tree of Renewal – Pastoral Symphony	32
The Silence of Deafness	33
Unfathomable – Piano Sonata No 32	34
Chopin	35
Nocturne – Mystery of Darkness	37
Raindrop Prelude	38
Nocturne – on the Causeway	39
Etude – the Singing Forest	40
Liszt	41
Concerto No 1 – Waterfront Memories	43
Consolation – it is more than this	44

Liebestraume – a Rhapsody	45
Years of Pilgrimage	46

Wagner — 47
- Parsifal – the Unasked Question — 49
- Parsifal – the Grail Quest — 50
- Parsifal – the Grail Chord – in 7s — 51
- Tristan – Intertwining Ivy — 52

Stanford — 53
- Blue Bird — 55
- I Never Left You – an Irish Rhapsody — 56
- Jetty of Broken Dreams — 57
- A Soft Day — 58

Delius — 59
- Sea Drift — 61
- Summer Night on the River — 62
- Eventyr – the Nowhere Key — 63
- Downriver — 64

Rachmaninov — 65
- Piano Concerto No. 2 in C Minor — 67
- Snakes and Ladders – a Prelude — 68
- Rossetti's Journey into Love — 69
- Breakout – Rhapsody on a Theme of Paganini — 70

Vaughan Williams — 73
- Sea Symphony — 75
- Pastoral Symphony — 76
- Explorers – the Singing Stars — 77
- Explorers – Beyond the Barrier — 78

Sculthorpe — 79
- Sun Music — 81
- Small Town — 82
- Misdirection to Lasseter's Reef — 83
- New Dawn — 84

Introduction

The Life River

Life is a river
a dawn wellspring beginning
coursing
over rough and smooth surfaces
from hidden sources
life giver, act of creation
over valleys outstretching
horizons broadening
day/night unfolding
into sunsets uncounted
crossing oceans in flood
and ebb unlimited
marking time's passing
in love with the beautiful
'passers-by'
a music of spirits
touching the sky
sacred in self and soul
unravelling memory's
temporal threads
re-weaving them
into eternity.

Hildegard of Bingen

The Sanctuary

Light my fire
'*O Ignis Spiritus Paracliti*'
spirit of prophecy
like an alpine wind's sharp blade
snow breath cold on lips and tongue
dispersing darkness
clarifying light's piercing
purifying raid
outwardly firing across
retinas unshielded

illumination's branded
self-denier's invocation,
perception's rowelling spur
inciting dreamers
inwardly to grow
in windward facing cells
opening onto mystery.

O Jerusalem
across horizons painting light
kill not the Prophets
challenging hopes falsified
behold
'The Signs of the Times'
over-rolling stone upthrust,
bells re-echoing history
flailing the dust of time's derision.

Illumination

Illumination,
when no more nuclear devastated
the coral atoll
centre and zenith, height and depth
is no more
the sacred land deconsecrated
a shore
made barren by a scorching wind
no store
of resentment from the conquered
a bitter toll
paid by hopes incinerated,
and illumination
'The Descent of the Dove'
opens the door
to unconditional, undemanding love
the Dove taking flight
into oneness
as sand slips through the hour glass
one, all, All and One.

Charles Williams – His Confession

Mind wings are veils parting
for the Dove's descent
slantwise darting
across peripheral visions
inherent in light emissions
dancing across the day
emerging
from spontaneous trances
awakened by the need
to pierce a blackness
falling outwards
onto undirected sight
but love
comes glowing into the world's
sunlit lower reaches
threatened
by this shadow-louring dark,
silent echo of a war in heaven
against the dissolution
of an all negating surd
until the Dove,
wings cloud-parting
lets me see this dark
as but a passing thing
beyond which
all is turned to gold

I have not sold, my love
nor could I give away
what is beyond all pricing.

Hildegard's Knowing

Love's patter-soft wind song
steals up on her
variously light and dark.

Initiation's spark
is a wing stirring vision
across moon paths glowing
like massed flowers
red, blue, white, gold
a flowing cascade,
a serenade
untoned yet singable
a power tameable
shining silver cool against black.

Escaping the rack
of reason, when dawn light
reveals Sophia companioning
the Dove descending
she knows herself
and wisdom.

J.S. Bach

Et In Arcadia Ego – a Musical Offering

Enter the heart zone
'Thy will be done'.
      Behold, know me by name!
Invoke the 'four and twenty elders'
      After, before, and in between
Name, purifying the motive
      Consciously moving in the game
Archangels on whose shoulders
Rests the Cosmos, with votive
Candles joyfully lit.
      Holding onto the seen and unseen
Against the outer dark
Direct clear insight fit
Intensified to spark
Agape, in devotion and release

Enter the heart zone
'Go forth in peace'
Overcome.

The Art of Fugue

Light mirroring, reflecting,
directing light's fugal melodies
takes flight between the columns
of the passing years
pattern based, chimes
outrunning times
serpentine, self revealing
in dark, or light-bursts
dazzling
out-flying the seeing
of a daunting splendour
like lightning
colour splintering
kaleidoscopic fantasies
sound, light, and rhythm's
interweaving exaltation
towards sun flares
manifesting outwardly
an inner light
the Sun behind the Sun's
light/sound visibly

and sound/light audibly
the Art of Fugue
incompletely human
template
for a temple in time
out of time transcending
time and centred
spiralling to the Zenith.

One Light – after Plato

One candle is enough
light off a cave wall
to set shadows leaping
illuminating the stall,
a sleeping place
for whatever caged in time
is out of time by reason
rhyme, or idealised imaginings
answering the simple question
hard to answer
and no time to pick
over the leavings
of momentary frivolities
challenging,
goading one riding the tiger
with an aristocratic soul
a desert persona
hearing the unheard
unguarded message.

A dust devil's
dissolving mandala
cyclones fear into non-existence
when light and time constant
only in their shape-shifting
timeless inconstancy
are memories dissolving
time into distance.

I Tego Arcana Dei – a Musical Offering

In darkness, walking towards light's

Turning point, time's wheeling ages
Encounter simplicities and insights
Growing from history's worn pages
Over generations, such delights

Angels accepting in service lovingly
Recall a pelican's sacrifice, and nurture
Candidates sun-fired, inspirationally
Arising like eagles, marking each creature
Named by Adam, knowing intimately
All the heart knows; but one lamed

      Beholden to a name
Dominical in poise, manning the breach
        After, before, and in between
Enemies notwithstanding and enflamed,
      Consciously moving in the game
Irradiating beyond time's outreach
        Holds to the seen and unseen.

Mozart

The Magic Flute – Persephone

Spring's flashing run is more
than 'The Wearing O' the Green'
Persephone
shaking night's foundations
foot-touching earth's dew sheen
unrolling a rainbow floral carpet
in her wake, activating
earth, water, airy, fiery elementals
and the Magic Flute
dropping silver tipped white trails
snail-bright but swifter
singing blood through veins,
challenging dark event horizons
the abyssal edge
where gods, clear-lighted, visible
lead on the Mysteries
penetrating the Green Man's
leaf shrouded gaze
unto the Sun unclouded, waiting,
his light blaze outer facing
the inner, unseen Sun.

Persephone
open the dawn-wide gate.

The Magic Flute – **Pamina and Tamino**

Serpent wrestler
on a darkened stage
Pamina's calling

seasonal floral dancing
stepping-stone crossing
the passing hours,
a jester in a rage of lures
chain-rattling
against the call to raising,
a matrix challenging
balancing, blazing
seven fired powers
counterbalancing
The Queen of the Night's
dazzling coloratura's
falsely promiscuous displays

the Magic Flute replays
white spirit voices
summoning the Wrestler
leaving a following trail
from midnight to sunrise
opening the Temple's gates
to the Archangel of the Sun.

Symphonic Jupiter

Rhythms are dancers
tricksters, chancers
teasers, daring
whirlpool destructive storms
and a red spot's pulsing
growing anger shrinking
before the heavens
'Rondo Alla Turca'
until a little leaven
leavens the orbiting mass
changing symphonically
into cosmic dancing
parodying rhythmic rites
when one man sees
Olympian Zeus
and does not die but laughs
penning a galactic finale
a scoped universal
uncustomary
unfashionable reversal,
a fugal peroration
bringing the cosmos
into one divinely circling
coda, eternally Mozart
at the top of his game.

A Mysterious Stranger

The street, a slow march echoer
is anonymity masked,
a commission even stranger
haunts a ranger of the soul
for peace, and the wounded heart
a behind the mask
overshadowing task,
an anomalistic
'*Requiem aeternum*
Dona eis Domine'

by chanters chorusing
a solemnity of pallbearers
and dread a heavy measure
darkening their slow foot tread.

'*Miserere nobis*',
a dark night soul's descent
into illusion
before Jacob's Ladder
rising to the stars
in polar circumambulation
unfinishes his requiem…

Beethoven

Storm Surge – from the 5th Symphony

A centred
sea/sky merging solitary wave rider
torn sail reefed
soars across undefinably vanishing horizons
the sea's ripped-off surface
lashing drooping clouds
morphing running waves into hills
leaping against falling skies
cyclonic fury blending air and water
a seething union
another state of being
the becoming
of an undiscriminating entity unstoppably
raising him storm battered
towards the centred eye
casting through the unchallengeable
spear-like balancing
self-awareness on the will to power
symbolically encompassing
an absolute intensity of mysteries
unleashing the unconquerable.

The Tree of Renewal – Pastoral Symphony

Elementally returning
to a coloured spontaneity
of earth and water,
a bottle brush red's
brief circus act
wind-flung sideways
on the turn
dance and dancer
firing as one
bowing when the wind slows
to a caress

the tree of renewal
reverts
to skeletal ordinariness
a draggle of thinly
undistinguished leaves
over skewed wood
yet not lifeless
in a spring-fire aftermath
just a stripped back
resignation
to the wisdom of necessity.

The Silence of Deafness

No more surging sounds
pitched, unpitched resonances
surf-wavelike terrors of delight
breaking the bonds of adversity

no more street-side footsteps intruding
clopping hooves and rumbling wheels
cross-matching the human banter
of an ordinary day

I am enrolled
in the University of Silence
unto life's evening
the dimming of the light
oncoming night
and darkness enclosing me
hearing, out of the air
voices, promptings, mind and will
training the inner ear to share
sounds echoing
round my soundless head
and, when I have passed
into the light
sounding across eternity.

Unfathomable – Piano Sonata No 32

Beyond bass-resonant
vibrato sonorities out-spacing
softly clashing harmonies
earth is a distant coin-gold disk
atoning, attuning
to the universal soul's swift
consonantal flight into infinity
passing Neptune in a moment
as light waves rippling
sparked gold/blue stippling
enlighten life's recessional
and bells are tolling
for a voyager
when lights gold winking
many million golden miles
and golden trees
in silence standing
many million golden years
on Betelgeuse
outlive Uranian magic
collapsing into dreams
and earthly bondage broken
is an eagle soaring to the sun.

Chopin

Nocturne – Mystery of Darkness

Your presence elevates
this mystery of darkness
an alchemy
of limitlessly timeless haunting
a dreamed recessional
following my searching
sensing-after quest
for beauty idealised
since first I saw
across a street light's pale
impersonality
cool bright in memory
yourself imprinted
on the edge of sight
a night-cut etching darkly
incommunicable
without the soft caress of hands
eyes touching lightly,
reminding me
our pathways need not be
cold stone, but carpeted
yet starlit glowing
through the night with love,
never alone.

Raindrop Prelude

A vaulted, dark,
raindrop haunting echo chamber
sombrely
percussively pianistic
resonates against stone
vibrating wire and wood

dream gatherers stark
oppressive,
echoes deep yet rising
into blackness
overhang
piercing a soaking
humid silence
like tipped arrows silver
slowed in flight
by febrile concentration
delirium their driver
penetrating

but love's mark
the stigmata
on love's healing hands
transforms the suffering.

Nocturne – on the Causeway

The cliffs stepped downwards
in black columned clusters
like fingers pointing northwards
into breaking waves,
I saw you standing
above a foam flecked sea
silhouetted against pearl grey clouds
painted across blue.

Vision and reality waited
recollecting a true silhouette
a perfect form imprinting
this magical moment
while light and shadow
counter-pointed gull calls
and parabolic arcs
of light tipped wings,
a time for passing by
like chiming, pealing bells
suspended in a blending
of perceptions.

Still the wind sings
serenading a different landscape
far from the one we knew
yet what I remember
is not, even by death
transcended but now
and always, unended.

Etude – the Singing Forest

Her swaying singing echoes
flashing, light sparking
surf the wind
in a forest Etude, lifting
wave surging, falling
vocalising harmonies
with a modifying
hammered wire tone
silvered piano merging
rendering leaf and branch
a hissing, sighing
musicality's responsorial psalm
outrun by running water-light's
pianistic touching
through dark, light,
storm and calm
a muse melodic spinning
from forest voices calling.

Liszt

Concerto No 1 – Waterfront Memories

Wind whips the waterfront
a grey road seaward stretches
iron railings frown above an estuary
and decorative souvenir shops
balance the scene's pianistic
virtuoso concerto sensations
across a summer morning's kites
dancing on air.

Ice cream and candy floss drifters
stroll andante moderato
in an off-river breeze
tickling senses with tide exposed
dark seaweed smell
as flitting sail triangles
bulge across the harbour.

Youthful, wild risk takers
climb barnacle encrusted
tide-wet pillars
a jetty their temple
step-piled pillars
its sanctuary columns
heedlessly assuming
'the luck of the draw'
on immortality's retrieval
from holiday passing hours
a once-in-a-while release
from customary control.

Consolation – it is more than this

Soul companionship is more
than form, voice, gesture,
ungraspable as cloud
rock permanent
in impermanence
a sudden recognition
fusing opposites
into simplicity
denying the double will
like Scotus Erigena
in a terse, defining
mutually linking
self sealing against
fin de siècle weariness
completing
the Yin/Yang hermetic union
above and below.

Liebestraume – a Rhapsody

I will be
in the aftermath of youth
your recollection in tranquillity
though controversial even in love.

Music is above blood ties
yet passion I know
fashion I emulate
sometimes
but neither do I trust
preferring wise dispassion

though eyes catch me still
in a net of desire's instability
because
when fingers touch
first ivory then flesh
all else is forgotten, until I wake
from *liebestraume*
in my rhapsodising mind
turning back from Eros
into music.

Years of Pilgrimage

Pianistic fingers scattering diamonds
catching lights of concert halls
jewellery, fixed, reflecting eyes
colours, tastings,
a blended wine of living essences
dissipated by vacant
unfamiliar rooms
and competition's déjà vu
for the well travelled
a heart's reliquary locked
and love's unravelled
attar of roses in scented memory's
silk, satin, touch, passion

'Vanity of vanities'
all is vanity's disillusion turning
to circumscribing trials of faith,
younger minds catching
wraiths of mythic arrogance
from Wagner's hero-cultic vision
tamed at last by Parsifal
and the Dove descending until
those years of pilgrimage
come full circle

RIP
Franz Liszt

Wagner

Parsifal – the Unasked Question

More substance than shadow
'The Fool on the Hill'
is innocence under open skies
or wandering leaf softened
sun/shadowed forest paths
all seasons a widow's
outcast son
until a white hart summons
this following fool through
sun and rain slanting
dark/lit networks
to retreating horizons
'The Fool on the Hill'
in a world going round
and round skylines
breaking over domes
and spires, insights
giving meaning
to gnosis in time
his cover yet unshaken
on the tracks of silence,

'Brother what ails thee?'

The world turns its back.

Parsifal – the Grail Quest

Hidden, stone-studded paths
and bloodstained feet
on pilgrim's mountain tracks
out-mark all ways
stormbound to greet
a stumbling
forest shelter search
for spaces networked by wet
slipping roots, in cold denial
of the heart's heat;

'Brother what ails thee?'

Harsh winds and rains out-beat
my tempo testing moods
between interludes
of birdsong day/night
mysteriously
'The Nightingale and the Rose'
temptation taunting
innocence unbroken
yet light unmasking
beyond the visible,
love's eyes seeing through
a wasteland of pain, because…
'The Grail serves the wounded King.'

Parsifal – the Grail Chord – in 7s

Kundalini Fire's sunset blood is sacrifice
the eagle rising and the pelican's self giving

by the flight of the Dove to the Sun
enlightenment, desire's food is mystery
and orange symbolically my light in living

by the wounding of the heart and the pierced brow
is sunrise yellow flaring, thriving,
lustrous over water in the spirit

because that which is, now, will run for eternity
green in renewal, calling from root to stem
for freedom from the heart's long winter

and along the blue sea/sky's road to inherit
detachment everlasting from material demerit
across a time space bridge with grace triumphant

in the sharpness of vision's eye firing
indigo, mediating blue and violet but neither

until Kether's Crown, a violet glory
giver of flowering enlightenment's
Grail Chord time/space sounding story
rises beyond the Ogdoad,

love's dart accepted; all is done.

Tristan – Intertwining Ivy

Love, is ivy climbing
sun/green glossed
into the light
intertwining
inseparably a shining
sun/moon essence
distilling
into the sunset
a grail fusion
when lovers lost
disinclining
the bonds of matter
reuniting
are perfectly inclining
unto twin selves
entwining
in the circle of eternity
one
forever.

Stanford

Blue Bird

Blue bird, singing light
crossing the sun's rays, rising
bright winging messenger
chanting the day's
'*Te Deum Laudamus*'
capture light on water
splintering into rainbow colours,
unshadow by a light-pulse wave
all senses, employ the mind
and singing heart, responding
slow, fast, lightning flashing
even superluminal
into the dawn's strong waking
where everything above,
below is NOW potentially
and always.

I Never Left You – an Irish Rhapsody

Mist and rain waltzing fitfully
over shallow inshore waters
shadow-cross my mind
and present time ghosts
like wild geese call me
half a world away

sun-struck, fluidly
dawn rising lark song
and heather humming
wind singing voices
are one with music
sun/brass blowing
light ringing St Patrick's Day.

I never left you
country of the heart
lit once against the dark
by wandering scholars
in rough weathered ruins
towers rounding skywards
and no mechanically
existential dreaming
to mask the sleepers voices
long forgotten
in time's relentless passing
where wild grasses grow
unheeded
over unvisited graves.

Jetty of Broken Dreams

Skeletally stark
against bloodshot light
jetty of broken dreams
uniformly dark
and statuesquely still
above a swiftly quiet
sneaking tide
oozing across a beach
shelving imperceptibly
towards the sea's
ebb/flow inevitability

ships no longer call
their shades time frozen
like film clips stopped
and insidious tidal flows
regress war's nemesis
or winter storms
in striking savagery
yet ghosts loom elusively
yards and masts imprinting
on dawn and sunset light
intangible reminders
of what was
and will not be again.

A Soft Day

The breeze is a wetly aromatic honey
a lip/tongue tasting amrita, transient
freedom outside the customary

a rain sweet sensing, drenching breath
mist soft, insistent yet bereft
of the imaginal beyond the temporary

'The grass is greener on the other side'
of death's gate, bright silver
speckled on a soft day offsetting
a flower/tree phantasmagoria

red, yellow, blue, white, orange, lately
enlightening like water falling
into scents, rose, jasmine, stocks, violet

a frangipani, oleander mix inviolate
itself infusing light thinned pearl veil-like
shifting soundlessly

what self is caressing through the mist?

Delius

Sea Drift

Below clouded shrouded cliff tops
loneliness
is the great Northern Diver
calling
into wind over water flows
sounding
distantly, spatially contemplative
overflowing
tidal surges, wind song and light
flared thinly, yet strongly
etched into colours sand-pale
weed-dark, stone greened-over
wet, shorelines pebble dashed
a cantilena
after storm and calm
for grey cloud-vapour drops
chanting soundlessly
falling onto the sea drift
echoing slowly, calling,
sky/sea swooping
instantly, luminously responsive
to a song-born urge's
primal knowing.

Summer Night on the River

A humming mayfly swarm,
a hovering river ballet's
shimmer-clouding serenade
baits fish rising to the catch
fin/scale silver in the evening light.

Red-slanting sun relays
night's promise
its gold-star masquerade
matching a sky black offset
slow flight star/moon rising
crossing over into setting
stretching a water-worldly
darkly sound-lit dreaming
and the infinite freedom
of a boat floating soundlessly
over light-fire sparks
above/below mirroring
a breeze's featherlike
barely perceptible touch
on a land/water nightscape's
sinuous melodic wandering's
endless transition.

Eventyr – the Nowhere Key

After nightfall
night black looming trees, tall under
darkness beyond shadowing, calling
silently distant star fires winking
around forest pillars like fairy lights
hearing, fearing inaudible spirits
pine needle dancing to forget
Loki the Trickster promising
light, beauty, love and dreaming
fulfilment beyond the dark water, and
a black-singing coral-eyed swan's
death-river destination
abjuring secretive
scheming shadow bonding
night trolls menacing…

All wait   for stone-turning
dawn light's breakout
the key to 'EREWHON'.

Downriver

North Country Sketches captured
autumnal wind songs
soughing in the trees
stripping protesting branches
tossing leaf-copper clouds
the confetti of an autumn wedding
let go long ago
shedding no benediction on
winter's frost-following show
and bleak memory strong,
so leave it.

Downriver is another country
lark ripple-singing
along the dawn's dew gleam,
an Appalachian Spring's
enraptured ringing summonses,
or orange groves illimitable
through night's soft parted curtain
glowing, unclouded, clouded,
unshrouded and released
into memory.

Rachmaninov

Piano Concerto No. 2 in C Minor

Love, more than memory
rose coloured by time
beyond music sable
silver, aspiring
and forest deep green
self-sings its passage
into autumn's yellow, red,
golden, in slant-sun glowing

history's leaf scattering
onto water running, bells
chiming, love's cable tow
late firing summer's energy's
dew bright sheen replaced
by wind tossed messages
foreknowing
a soft treading winter's onset
the showing of a mystery,
sun/shadow silences
overpassing hills, imaging
soul flight, soul's light
into winter and beyond.

Wait for me
by the 'Doors of Perception'
with love,
not as a rhapsody
but a knowing ultimate
in height and depth
leading me on through
winter jasmine's flowering
into spring.

Snakes and Ladders – a Prelude

Rungs and staves
are all the virtues
balanced
tightrope poised
attained
or understood
when falling water laves
tired feet and love
seeks not from labour
to be free
when hearts disclosed
may be
from fear released
greeting companions
on the road
where is no ending
or beginning
just love to goad
the souls and spirits
whom love saves
enclosing
for opening into light.

Rossetti's Journey into Love

Love is a memory after brief sleep
with pre-dawn paleness
infiltrating the eastern sky
gradually revealing shapes
through night's soft-footed steal away

a waking trance
before the day's unfolding
a knowing
when curtains are drawn back
her hair across white pillows
will glow like fire in answer
to the sun's strong challenge
his Mary Magdalene
mistress of his 'House of Life'
before light-fired memory
shadowed by foreknowing
is still, the cloud's unknowing
yet a foreboding
claiming her as '*Beata Beatrix*'
a life unlinking
from the chain of time.

'Love her, Dante Gabriel
past youth's long-summering
long remembered "Silent Noon"
into the everlasting light.'

Breakout – Rhapsody on a Theme of Paganini

Sun on silver might be white fire splendour
were the sheen elsewhere than razor wire.

Nonconformity
is wild geese in flight
by steel, sun, cold, heat and distance
wing clipped.

Do petals wind stripped
drop for the defeated,
muffled drum thunders complement
blossoms falling on the dead?

Strife's mental infirmity
is unreality's dread
building empires of the unnatural
yet freedom's signification
is a backwards unravelling
forward into tapestried forms
desiring, storming the barricades
under a blue sky skin.

On distant shores
sand swirls and rain showers thin
counterpoint scorching sunbursts.

The brave empower their confraternity
whenever they cut, or impulse rips
this wire screen
while the sidereal clock slow/fast
time mirrors the seasonal paradox.

Dare we, in equinox or solstice modes
demand a preference for tolerance?

Imagine not the locked gate
trapping freedom's aspirations
and refugee hopes behind
the inference of lies living, as they do
outside the prison of conformity.

Vaughan Williams

Sea Symphony

The sea, is all seasons unto itself
beyond climate mystique's
light, dark asymmetrical
shaded rhapsody, occasionally
St Elmo's Fire sparked
blue/grey/green faceted moods
a variously orchestrated
cosmic symphony.

A wave-tossed deck spray slippery
repositions constantly,
wet rope roughness
and a winch's metal cold touch
tool-up, confronting shadow-sided
long-sloped rollers
yellow/white foam crested
momentously
neither cruel nor kind
just the sea.

Sky gazing is denied
for sunless/starless day/night
lifeline dependents imposed upon,
defied by restrictive uncertainties
strained rigging
threat bulging sail
swinging compass needle
wind howl wave break
and eyes salt-spume stung tired,
a relentless harrowing.

Pastoral Symphony

No Last Post or Reveille

a melisma palely gilded
trumpet clear
yet singing a falling
through night long watching
into the morning

no Lark Ascending
but frost touched
winter silence
coldly weakening a shining
silver crystallising,
a trodden grassed upward way
towards hilltop ruins
black, broken, appealing
against a day's white flaring
hard edged rising.

Light haunts, unblessing
this shattered pile's
lingering
sanctified long memory's
Pastoral Symphony.

Explorers – the Singing Stars

Stars no longer heaven bound
descend through lengthening light
seaward singing,
fiery, comet tailed
white falling spectaculars
leaving the macrocosm
racing down before
the curtaining Barrier
released from bondage
to the Great Year's wheel
flame-bending into forms
unseen on earth
yet summoning earth voices
calling the last temptation into song,
sine-toned breathing
pan flute-like chanting
serpentine melismas flowing

'Turn back from the unknown
beyond known things
turn back into heat, cold,
cool thinking, hot desire
turn back from lilies
in a shrinking sea
turn back into the fading, turn…'

Explorers – Beyond the Barrier

Water now sweet is almost light
passing endless dawn's
'Sundoor at World's End'
a condition of unconcern
with possessing
never to see again the falling leaf
the dying fire
time ebbing like the tide

feet touch sand cool and lilies white
spread round their boat
from centre to horizon.

Bells no longer chime
the regulated hours
old songs beyond hearing
cannot recall those long passed on
their grounded boat unmoored
shorn of necessity
sails idle, rigging slack,
unworn in timelessness.

New songs will rhyme them in
unheard before their passing
leaving one world as they entered it
alone in mist white rising,
a shining before the entrance
and no backward looking
after the unknowing.

Veil-soft radiance
clouds their passing until lifted
beyond the Barrier.

Sculthorpe

Sun Music

Sun-strong splendour
drew from him
a pride of influences
hot angularities of melody
not Waltzing Matilda
brass and bronze clashing
a hymn to differences
confluences
a haunting threnody
for the lion and the lamb
with Asia calling
blending with eucalypts
in orchestral dioramas
estranging
colonising dreamers
mind-echoing awhile
a light etched song's
red centred sacredness
landscape shaped
evoked by bell, gamelan
and vocal synthesising
with smoking leaves creating
thought forms running free
pioneering pathways
through the years.

Small Town

The Last Post, almost…

a distant sigh side-swept by the dawn wind

one last train leaving the station with no show
and a following silence having nothing to bestow
but weeds colonising the tracks;

a cry in the dark?

Can 'Small Town' abide a new dawn
of hope thread thinned, prevaricating,
like old photographs turning sepia
with regret?

'Small Town: is there a gain in remembering?'

Misdirection to Lasseter's Reef

Dreaming dust thirst crazy
seeing fools gold sunstone glinting
or lazily perhaps, bought and sold
in the market place, hinting
at what cannot be washed clean
by inertial excuses
philosophically ambiguous,
memorialising, hazily scheming
and dreaming for results
predictably the same as ever
when sensibly tame nay-sayers
having my best interests at heart
reject my unseen endeavour

'Time gentlemen please!
Raise your glasses cautiously
mean spirited scavengers for gold

'my coda's secret alchemy
is misdirection,
liberation in extremis,
inspiration's empathy.'

New Dawn

Eastward
above wing-white sails over water
new dawn
is a blazing gold arc burning
above a hot horizon
summoning
a sunward facing mantra's
bird-calling chorus lines
resounding
to human interactions rising
from tree and roof
reaching a concave morning sky
merging
a sun/white pallor into blue
cloudlessly
as harbour city dreams
sprawl coloured in refractions
and that wide curving bridge
a cast black
vision of the possible
challenges mirage disturbing light
beholding
the meridian potential
of the sunrise moment…

NOT THE END

www.ingramcontent.com/pod-product-compliance
Lightning Source LLC
Chambersburg PA
CBHW062145100526
44589CB00014B/1689